The Big Day!
Moving House

Nicola Barber

WAYLAND

First published in 2008 by Wayland

Copyright © Wayland 2008

Wayland
338 Euston Road
London NW1 3BH

Wayland Australia
Level 17/207 Kent Street
Sydney, NSW 2000

Editor: Camilla Lloyd
Designer: Elaine Wilkinson
Picture Researcher: Kathy Lockley

Picture Acknowledgments: The author and publisher would like to thank the following for their pictures to be reproduced in this publication: Cover photograph: Ariel Skelley/Corbis; Alan Powdrill/Taxi/Getty Images: 8; Altrendo Images/Getty Images: 7; Andy Crawford/Dorling Kindersley/Getty Images: 16, 24; Ariel Skelley/Corbis: 17; Chris Howes/Wild Places Photography/Alamy Images: 5; Comstock Select/Corbis: 15; DAJ/Getty Images: 18; Dave Cameron/Alamy Images: 9, 10; Fabio Cordoso/zefa/Corbis: 21; Horizon International Images Limited/Alamy Images: 14; Juan Silva/The Image Bank/Getty Images: 1, 6; Leslie Garland Picture Library/Alamy Images: 20; Reg Charity/Corbis: 21; Tim Pannell/Corbis: 13; Tom & Dee Ann McCarthy/Corbis: 19; Yellow Dog Productions/The Image Bank/Getty Images: 11.

British Library Cataloguing in Publication Data:
Barber, Nicola
  Moving house. - (The big day)
  1. Moving, Household - Juvenile literature
  I. Title
  648.9

ISBN: 978 0 7502 5365 9

Printed in China

Wayland is a division of Hachette Children's Books, an Hachette Livre UK company

Contents

 Time to move

You are moving house. Outside your old house there is a sign that says 'SOLD'.

What will moving house be like?

Mum and Dad may have taken you to see your new house already. You might even have chosen your new room.

It is sad to leave your old house, but it is exciting to be going somewhere new.

Getting ready

Before moving day, it's a good idea to sort out your toys and games. There may be some that you would like to give away.

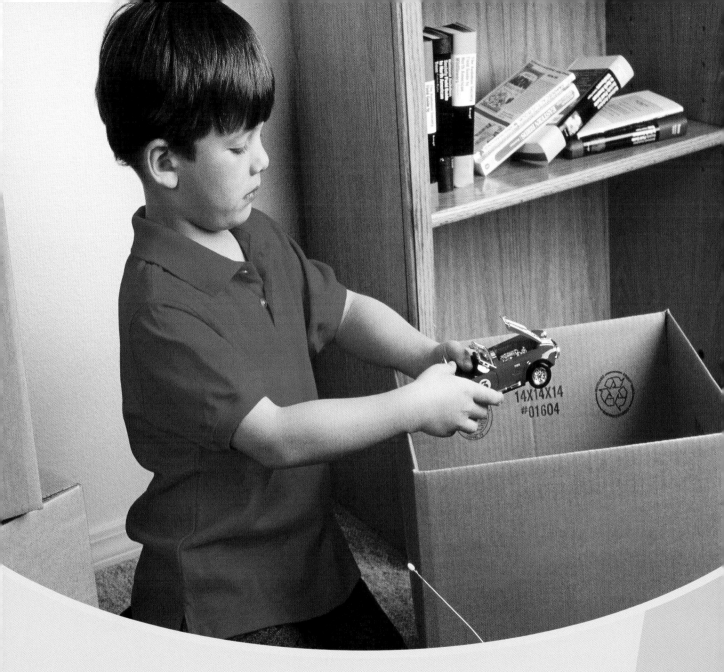

Your Mum and Dad help you to take down the pictures in your room. Then it's time to pack everything into big cardboard boxes.

Moving day

On moving day the removal truck arrives early. Do you think all the furniture and boxes in your house will fit inside the truck?

The truck looks huge when it's empty.
Everything gets loaded in – even your bikes.
You can help with some of the smaller boxes.

Saying goodbye

When the removal truck is full, your old house is empty. The rooms look very odd without all the furniture. It's time to say goodbye to your old house.

You say goodbye to your friends and neighbours too. You can keep in touch with your friends, and they can come and visit you at your new house.

Staying overnight

If your new house is a long way from your old one you might have quite a long journey.

You might have to stay overnight with friends, or maybe with your grandparents. Remember to pack your overnight things and your favourite toy, so that they don't go into the removal truck!

Your new house

It's exciting to see your new house. All the rooms are empty and it feels a bit strange at first.

Soon the removal truck arrives and your furniture and boxes start to fill up the rooms.

It looks a mess, but it will get better when
the furniture is in the right place and you
can start to unpack the boxes.

Unpacking

You can think about where to put your furniture in your new room. Now you can unpack your clothes and books, toys and games.

You can help your family with the unpacking
in the other rooms too.

First night

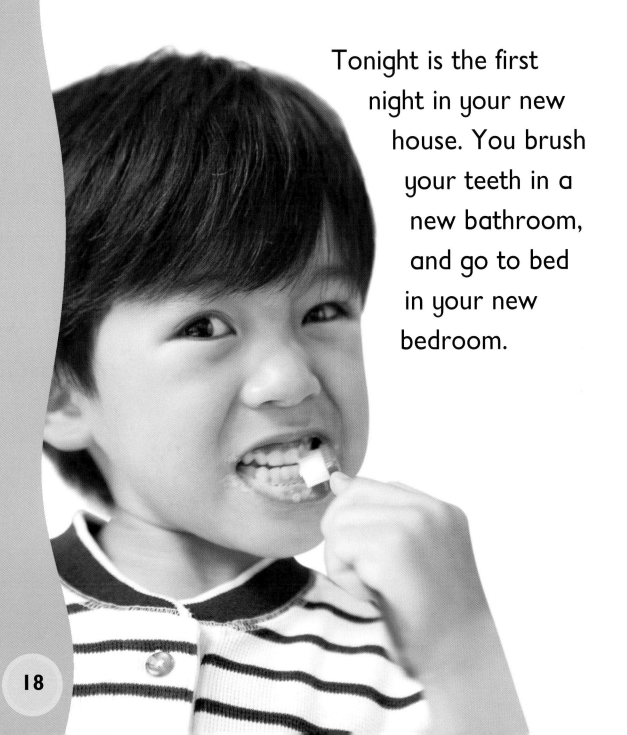

Tonight is the first night in your new house. You brush your teeth in a new bathroom, and go to bed in your new bedroom.

There are different sounds and different smells in your new house. Your parents are close by if you need them.

Exploring

Now it's time to start exploring your new neighbourhood. Is there a park near your new house? Are there any shops?

Soon you could be starting at a new school. You can make new friends, and you will still have your old friends too.

Enjoy your new home!

Moving house words

If you are writing about moving house these are some of the words you might need.

Bedroom

Neighbour

Box

Neighbourhood

Empty

Packing

Exploring

Removal truck

Furniture

Sold

House

Unpacking

Further information

Books

I Want That Room!: Moving House by Jen Green, Wayland, 2000

Lucy's New House (First Experiences) by Barbara Taylor Cork, School Speciality Publishing, 2002

Moving House (Usborne First Experiences) by Anne Civardi, Usborne Publishing, 2005

We're Moving House (First Time Stories) by Heather Maisner, Kingfisher Books, 2004

For parents

Moving with Kids: 25 Ways to Ease Your Family's Transition to a New Home by Lori Collins Burgan, Harvard Common Press, 2007

Websites for parents

http://www.helpiammoving.com/moving_house/moving_with_children.php

http://www.familiesonline.co.uk/index.php/article/articleview/283/1/27/

http://www.netdoctor.co.uk/health_advice/facts/movinghouse.htm

http://www.bbc.co.uk/parenting/q_and_a/movinghousechildren.shtml

http://www.babyworld.co.uk/features/movinghome1.asp

Index

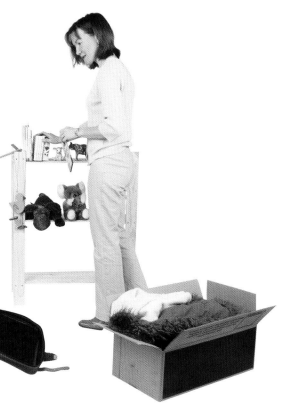